slow cooker
everything!

From the editors of
TASTE OF THE SOUTH®

hm | books

slow cooker
everything!

Hoffman Media
1900 International Park Drive, Suite 50
Birmingham, Alabama 35243
hoffmanmedia.com

ISBN # 978-1-940772-46-2
Printed in China

contents

introduction

IT'S NOT OFTEN THAT A KITCHEN APPLIANCE CAN CLAIM A PLACE IN AMERICAN HISTORY. That's not such a bizarre notion when you're talking about the slow cooker, however. Popularized in the 1970s, this compact countertop appliance quickly revolutionized the way people made dinner. Almost 50 years later, it's still influencing the way we cook.

The slow cooker's popularity surged at a turning point in American history, when women entered the work force in record numbers. More than half of these women were mothers with school-age children. Working mothers, especially in the South, quickly embraced the convenience and versatility of the slow cooker. It enabled them to hold down a full-time job and still come home to a hot meal at the end of the day. Today's innovations—from removable inserts that go from slow cooker to table to multi-function models that can also serve as pressure cookers and steamers—have made the slow cooker an even more indispensable kitchen appliance. At the end of the day, American families still depend on it to help bring everyone together at the dinner table.

We've packed this book with some of our favorite slow cooker recipes—from traditional pot roasts to stellar cakes and fudge. Prep the vegetables in the morning, and come home to a steaming pot of Southern Minestrone in the evening (page 83). Nestle a couple of spice-rubbed whole chickens on a bed of onions, and let your slow cooker work its magic. Or experiment with making your own homemade ketchup (page 127). Don't worry that some of these recipes make a lot; that just means there will be enough leftovers to make dinner the next day.

And be sure to save room for dessert—from Pineapple-Strawberry Upside Down Cake to warm and gooey Cinnamon Rolls—you'll be amazed at the delicious tricks your slow cooker can do.

Keep it low, slow, and deliciously simple!

The Editors of **Taste of the South**

Slow Cooker SUPPERS

NO TIME TO COOK? THINK AGAIN. LEAN ON YOUR SLOW COOKER
FOR HEARTY MAIN DISHES (AND DELICIOUS LEFTOVERS)
WHILE YOU WHIP UP OUR SUPER-FAST SIDES.

MAIN DISH

ON THE MENU

Main Dish
Slow Cooker
Chicken

Easy Sides
Roasted Red Potatoes
with Herbs

Easy Roasted Vegetables

Leftovers
Poppy Seed
Chicken Casserole

Easy Chicken
and Dumplings

Slow Cooker Chicken

Want an even crispier skin? Place the chicken under the broiler for 3 to 4 minutes after it cooks.

MAKES 1 WHOLE CHICKEN

2   tablespoons olive oil
1   tablespoon ground
     black pepper
2   teaspoons kosher salt
1   teaspoon smoked paprika
½   teaspoon onion powder
½   teaspoon garlic powder
1   (4-pound) whole chicken
4   small yellow onions, peeled

1. In a small bowl, stir together oil, pepper, salt, paprika, onion powder, and garlic powder; rub mixture over chicken.
2. In the bottom of a 6-quart slow cooker, place onions. Place chicken on onions.
3. Cover and cook on high for 4 hours, or until a meat thermometer inserted in thickest portion registers 165°. Let stand for 10 minutes before serving.

Roasted Red Potatoes with Herbs

MAKES ABOUT 4 SERVINGS

4 cups quartered small red potatoes
2 teaspoons olive oil
1 teaspoon chopped fresh thyme
1 teaspoon chopped fresh parsley
½ teaspoon kosher salt
½ teaspoon ground black pepper
2 teaspoons fresh lemon juice

1. Preheat oven to 350°. Line a rimmed baking sheet with foil.
2. In a large bowl, stir together potatoes, oil, thyme, parsley, salt, and pepper. Spread in an even layer on prepared pan.
3. Bake until potatoes are tender, about 35 minutes. Drizzle with lemon juice.

Easy Roasted Vegetables

MAKES ABOUT 4 SERVINGS

½ (12-ounce) package fresh
  broccoli florets
½ (10-ounce) package fresh
  cauliflower florets
½ cup chopped pecans
2 teaspoons olive oil
½ teaspoon kosher salt
¼ teaspoon ground black pepper

1. Preheat oven to 350°. Line a rimmed baking sheet with foil.
2. In a large bowl, stir together broccoli and remaining ingredients. Spread in an even layer on prepared pan.
3. Bake until tender, about 20 minutes.

Poppy Seed Chicken Casserole

*Have extra leftover Slow Cooker Chicken? Make this casserole
and freeze it—you'll thank yourself later.*

MAKES 4 TO 6 SERVINGS

¼ cup unsalted butter
¼ cup all-purpose flour
2¼ cups whole milk
3 cups chopped Slow Cooker
  Chicken (recipe on page 13)
¼ cup sour cream
1 tablespoon poppy seeds
1 teaspoon white wine vinegar
¼ teaspoon kosher salt
¼ teaspoon ground black pepper
1 cup crushed buttery
  round crackers

1. Preheat oven to 350°. Spray a 1½-quart baking dish with cooking spray.

2. In a large saucepan, melt butter over medium-high heat. Add flour, whisking until smooth. Add milk, whisking occasionally, until mixture begins to boil and thicken, about 10 minutes. Stir in chicken, sour cream, poppy seeds, vinegar, salt, and pepper. Spread evenly in prepared dish. Top with crackers.

3. Bake until hot and bubbly, about 20 minutes.

Easy Chicken and Dumplings

You can pull this meal together quickly thanks to frozen dumplings and leftover chicken.

MAKES ABOUT 4 SERVINGS

¼ cup unsalted butter
1 cup chopped yellow onion
1 cup chopped celery
1 cup chopped carrot
¼ cup all-purpose flour
2 (32-ounce) containers chicken broth
½ (32-ounce) package frozen dumplings, broken in thirds*
4 cups shredded Slow Cooker Chicken (recipe on page 13)
1 tablespoon chopped fresh thyme
1 tablespoon chopped fresh parsley

1. In a large Dutch oven, melt butter over medium-high heat. Add onion, celery, and carrot. Cook, stirring frequently, until tender, about 6 minutes. Add flour; cook, stirring constantly, 2 minutes. Stir in broth; bring to a boil.

2. Add frozen dumplings in batches, stirring to keep dumplings from sticking to bottom of pan. Bring back to a boil; reduce heat to medium-low. Cover and simmer, stirring occasionally, until dumplings are tender, about 30 minutes. Add chicken, thyme, and parsley; cook for 10 minutes more.

We used Mary B's.

ON THE MENU

Main Dish
Slow Cooker
Pasta Sauce

Easy Side
Quick and Easy Salad
Pull-Apart Garlic Bread

Leftovers
Stuffed Peppers
Easy Skillet Pizza

Slow Cooker Pasta Sauce

This simple sauce isn't just perfect for pasta—we love it as a pizza sauce, too.

MAKES ABOUT 12 CUPS

2   pounds lean ground beef
1   pound Italian sausage,
    casings removed
2   tablespoons olive oil
3   tablespoons tomato paste
2   tablespoons balsamic vinegar
8   sprigs fresh basil
2   garlic cloves, minced
2   (28-ounce) cans whole
    tomatoes, crushed
1   (28-ounce) can crushed
    tomatoes
½   teaspoon crushed red pepper
3   teaspoons kosher salt
1   teaspoon ground black pepper
1   pound cooked pasta
Garnish: grated Parmesan cheese,
    fresh basil

1. In a large nonstick skillet, cook ground beef and sausage over medium heat, stirring occasionally, until browned and crumbly, 6 to 8 minutes; drain.

2. In a 6-quart slow cooker, stir together cooked beef mixture, oil, tomato paste, vinegar, basil, garlic, tomatoes, red pepper, salt, and black pepper. Cover and cook on low for 8 hours.

3. To serve, spoon 4 cups pasta sauce over cooked pasta. Garnish with Parmesan and basil, if desired.

Quick and Easy Salad with Lemon Dressing

MAKES 6 TO 8 SERVINGS

1 head iceberg lettuce, torn into pieces
2 cups arugula
½ cup chopped tomato
¼ cup sliced red onion
¼ cup pitted Kalamata olives
¼ cup red wine vinegar
½ teaspoon lemon zest
2 tablespoons fresh lemon juice
2 teaspoons honey
½ teaspoon stone-ground mustard
½ teaspoon ground black pepper
½ teaspoon kosher salt
⅓ cup olive oil

1. In a large bowl, combine lettuce, arugula, tomato, onion, and olives.
2. In a medium bowl, whisk together remaining ingredients. Drizzle salad with Lemon Dressing just before serving.

Pull-Apart Garlic Bread

MAKES 6 TO 8 SERVINGS

⅓ cup unsalted butter
1 large clove garlic, minced
¼ cup chopped fresh parsley
1 (13.8-ounce) can refrigerated pizza crust

1. Preheat oven to 425°. Line an 8x4-inch loaf pan with parchment paper.

2. In a small saucepan, cook butter, garlic, and parsley over medium heat until butter melts. Remove from heat.

3. On a lightly floured surface, roll crust into a 21x12-inch rectangle. Brush with half of butter mixture. Using a knife, cut dough into 12 (3½-inch) squares. Fold each square in half; place cut side down in prepared pan. Repeat with remaining squares.

4. Bake until golden brown, about 15 minutes. Brush with remaining butter mixture. Serve warm.

Stuffed Peppers

Slow Cooker Pasta Sauce makes these cheesy peppers easy to whip up for a make-ahead supper.

MAKES ABOUT 6 SERVINGS

1½ **cups Slow Cooker Pasta Sauce (recipe on page 21)**
⅓ **cup cooked white rice**
1 **cup shredded Colby-Jack cheese, divided**
6 **large green bell peppers**

1. Preheat oven to 350°. Line a 13x9-inch baking pan with foil.

2. In a medium bowl, stir together Slow Cooker Pasta Sauce, rice, and ½ cup cheese.

3. Cut 1 inch off top of each pepper; discard stems, seeds, and membranes. Spoon rice mixture into peppers; transfer to prepared pan.

4. Bake 25 minutes. Sprinkle with remaining ½ cup cheese. Bake until cheese melts, about 5 minutes.

Easy Skillet Pizza

The rich and meaty leftover sauce makes this deep-dish pizza divine.

MAKES 6 TO 8 SERVINGS

1½ cups Slow Cooker Pasta Sauce (recipe on page 21)
4 teaspoons olive oil, divided
½ large yellow onion, sliced
1 (8-ounce) package sliced mushrooms
½ cup sliced pepperoni
1 (16-ounce) bag fresh pizza dough, at room temperature
7 slices provolone cheese
¼ cup shredded fresh basil
½ cup shredded mozzarella cheese

1. Preheat oven to 425°.

2. In a small saucepan, heat Slow Cooker Pasta Sauce over medium heat, stirring occasionally, until sauce thickens, 3 to 5 minutes. Set aside.

3. In a 10-inch cast-iron skillet, heat 2 teaspoons oil over medium heat. Add onion; cook, stirring occasionally, until lightly browned, about 5 minutes. Remove from skillet. Add mushrooms; cook until browned and tender, about 3 minutes. Remove from skillet. Add pepperoni; cook until lightly browned, 1 to 2 minutes. Remove from skillet; let drain on paper towels. Wipe skillet clean.

4. Place skillet over medium heat; drizzle with remaining 2 teaspoons oil. On a lightly floured surface, roll pizza dough into an 11-inch circle. Carefully press dough into bottom and up sides of skillet. Add provolone in a single layer; top with onion, mushroom, and pepperoni. Sprinkle with basil and mozzarella.

5. Bake 8 minutes. Reduce heat to 350°. Bake until crust is browned, 10 to 12 minutes more. Let stand for 15 minutes before slicing.

KITCHEN TIP

You can find fresh pizza dough in the deli section of your grocery store.

ON THE MENU

Main Dish
Classic Pot Roast

Easy Sides
Broccoli Salad with
Bacon and Pecans

Sour Cream
Mashed Potatoes

Leftovers
Pot Roast Pot Pie

Pot Roast Po' Boys

Classic Pot Roast

Add a side of mashed potatoes and this pot roast is complete.

MAKES 5 TO 6 SERVINGS

1 cup all-purpose flour

1 tablespoon plus ½ teaspoon
kosher salt, divided

1 teaspoon ground black pepper

1 (5- to 6-pound) beef chuck
roast, halved

2 tablespoons canola oil

1 large yellow onion, sliced
(about 2 cups)

1 (8-ounce) package sliced
mushrooms

1½ cups ketchup

1 cup beef broth

1 (1-ounce) package
onion soup mix

2 tablespoons red wine vinegar

½ teaspoon garlic powder

1. In a 13x9-inch pan, stir together flour, 1 tablespoon salt, and pepper. Dredge each half of beef in flour mixture.

2. In a large cast-iron skillet, heat oil over medium-high heat. Cook beef until browned on all sides, about 4 minutes per side. Transfer to a 6-quart slow cooker.

3. Add remaining ½ teaspoon salt, onion, and remaining ingredients to slow cooker. Cover and cook on low for 10 hours, or on high for 6½ hours or until tender.

4. Skim excess fat from gravy. Serve gravy with pot roast. Reserve remaining gravy for leftovers.

Broccoli Salad with Bacon and Pecans

MAKES ABOUT 10 SERVINGS

8   cups chopped broccoli
(2 large heads)
½   cup diced red onion
½   cup chopped pecans
4   slices cooked bacon, crumbled
½   cup sweetened dried
cranberries
¾   cup mayonnaise
1½   tablespoons Dijon mustard
1½   tablespoons apple
cider vinegar
2   teaspoons sugar
1   teaspoon kosher salt
¼   teaspoon ground black pepper

1. In a large bowl, combine broccoli, onion, pecans, bacon, and cranberries.

2. In a small bowl, whisk together mayonnaise and remaining ingredients. Pour dressing over broccoli mixture, stirring to combine. Refrigerate until ready to serve.

EASY SIDE

Sour Cream Mashed Potatoes

MAKES ABOUT 8 CUPS

3 pounds Yukon gold potatoes, peeled and quartered
1 clove garlic
3 tablespoons unsalted butter, divided
½ cup whole milk
1 (8-ounce) container sour cream
1 teaspoon kosher salt
Pinch ground black pepper

1. In a large Dutch oven, place potatoes and garlic; add water to cover. Bring to a boil over high heat; reduce to medium-low. Simmer until tender, about 10 minutes. Drain.
2. Return potatoes to pan; add 2 tablespoons butter, milk, sour cream, salt, and pepper. Mash to desired consistency. Top with remaining 1 tablespoon butter.

Pot Roast Pot Pie

A comforting pot pie is the perfect way to end a winter day.

MAKES ABOUT 6 SERVINGS

4 tablespoons unsalted butter
¼ cup all-purpose flour
1½ cups reserved Classic Pot Roast gravy (recipe on page 29)
1 cup beef broth
2 cups shredded Classic Pot Roast (recipe on page 29)
1 (10-ounce) package frozen peas and carrots mix
1 tablespoon chopped fresh thyme
½ teaspoon kosher salt
Pinch ground black pepper
½ (17.3-ounce) box frozen puff pastry sheets, thawed (1 sheet)
1 large egg, beaten

1. Preheat oven to 375°.

2. In a 10-inch cast-iron skillet, melt butter over medium heat. Whisk in flour; cook for 1 minute. Stir in reserved gravy, broth, Classic Pot Roast, vegetables, thyme, salt, and pepper. Bring to a boil, stirring frequently, until thickened, 3 to 5 minutes. Remove from heat.

3. On a lightly floured surface, unfold pastry sheet; roll into a 12-inch square. Place pastry over skillet. Using scissors, cut corners from pastry to create a circle. Cut 4 small vents in pastry; brush with egg.

4. Bake until pastry is golden brown, about 20 minutes.

Pot Roast Po' Boys

This New Orleans classic is the next best thing to a trip to the Big Easy.

MAKES ABOUT 4 SERVINGS

4   **tablespoons unsalted butter, softened**

2   **(12-inch) loaves French bread, halved and split lengthwise**

4   **tablespoons mayonnaise**

4   **teaspoons whole grain mustard**

2   **cups shredded Classic Pot Roast, warmed (recipe on page 29)**

Garnish: shredded lettuce, sliced tomatoes, dill pickle chips, reserved Pot Roast gravy

1. Heat a griddle over medium-high heat. Spread butter on inside of bread. Cook bread, split side down, until toasted, about 4 minutes. Remove from heat.

2. Spread each loaf with mayonnaise and mustard. Top with Classic Pot Roast. Garnish with lettuce, tomato, pickles, and gravy, if desired.

ON THE MENU

Main Dish	*Easy Sides*	*Leftovers*
Slow Cooker Brisket	Classic Coleslaw	Brisket Tacos
	Skillet Baked Beans	Quick Brisket Chili

Slow Cooker Brisket

Chile powder and smoked paprika give this brisket the smoky flavor you crave without having to fire up the grill.

MAKES 4 TO 6 SERVINGS

2   tablespoons canola oil
1   (4-pound) beef brisket
2½   teaspoons kosher salt, divided
¾   teaspoon ground black pepper, divided
2   cups chopped yellow onion
1   cup beef broth
½   cup ketchup
1   teaspoon ancho chile powder
1   teaspoon smoked paprika
½   teaspoon ground cumin

1. In a large skillet, heat oil over medium-high heat. Trim excess fat from brisket, leaving about a ½-inch layer. Season brisket with 1½ teaspoons salt and ½ teaspoon pepper. Add brisket to skillet. Cook until browned on both sides, about 2 minutes per side. Transfer to a 6-quart slow cooker, fat side up.

2. Add onion to skillet; cook until lightly browned, about 2 minutes. Add to slow cooker.

3. In a medium bowl, whisk together broth, ketchup, chile powder, paprika, cumin, remaining 1 teaspoon salt, and remaining ¼ teaspoon pepper; pour over brisket.

4. Cover and cook on low for 10 hours or until tender, or on high for 6½ hours. Place brisket, fat side up, on a cutting board; let stand for 15 minutes before slicing. Skim excess fat from gravy. Serve gravy with brisket.

Classic Coleslaw

MAKES 6 TO 8 SERVINGS

8	cups thinly sliced green cabbage
1	cup shredded carrot
½	cup sliced red onion
½	cup chopped green onion
¼	cup distilled white vinegar
2	tablespoons canola oil
1	teaspoon sugar
1	teaspoon salt
¼	teaspoon ground black pepper
¼	teaspoon celery seeds

1. In a medium bowl, combine cabbage, carrot, red onion, and green onion. In a small bowl, whisk together vinegar and remaining ingredients. Pour over cabbage mixture, stirring to combine. Let stand for 30 minutes before serving. Cover and refrigerate for up to 2 days.

Skillet Baked Beans

MAKES 4 TO 6 SERVINGS

4 slices bacon
⅔ cup chopped yellow onion
½ cup chopped green bell pepper
½ cup chopped celery
1 (15-ounce) can pinto beans,
  drained and rinsed
1 (15-ounce) can navy beans,
  drained and rinsed
1 (15-ounce) can light red kidney
  beans, drained and rinsed
1½ cups barbecue sauce

1. Preheat oven to 350°.

2. In a 10-inch cast-iron skillet, cook bacon over medium heat until crisp. Remove bacon, and let drain on paper towels, reserving drippings in pan. Add onion, bell pepper, and celery to pan; cook over medium-high heat until lightly browned, about 4 minutes. Stir in beans and barbecue sauce. Top with bacon.

3. Bake until bubbly, about 25 minutes.

Brisket Tacos

Leftover brisket adds a little Southern twist to this easy weeknight supper.

MAKES ABOUT 4 SERVINGS

3   cups chopped Slow Cooker
    Brisket (recipe on page 37)
1½ teaspoons ground cumin
1   teaspoon kosher salt
2   tablespoons canola oil
9   (6-inch) corn tortillas
Chopped green onion, chopped
    white onion, chopped fresh
    cilantro, sliced radish,
    lime wedges, and hot sauce,
    to serve

1. In a medium bowl, toss together brisket, cumin, and salt. In a 10-inch skillet, heat oil over medium-high heat. Add brisket; cook until browned, about 3 minutes, stirring frequently.

2. Warm tortillas according to package directions. Spoon Slow Cooker Brisket over tortillas. Serve with onions, cilantro, radish, lime wedges, and hot sauce.

Quick Brisket Chili

This comforting chili will fill up even the hungriest diner.

MAKES 5 TO 6 SERVINGS

1   tablespoon canola oil
1   cup chopped yellow onion
2   cloves garlic, minced
2   cups beef broth
2   cups (½-inch) cubed
     Slow Cooker Brisket (recipe on
     page 37)
1½   cups crushed tomatoes
2   (15-ounce) cans pinto beans,
     drained and rinsed
1   (15-ounce) can black beans,
     drained and rinsed
1   (4-ounce) can mild chopped
     green chiles
2   tablespoons tomato paste
1½   teaspoons kosher salt
2   teaspoons ancho chile powder
1½   teaspoons ground cumin
Garnish: shredded Monterey Jack
     cheese, sliced fresh jalapeño
     pepper
Tortilla chips, to serve

1. In a small Dutch oven, heat oil over medium-high heat. Add onion; cook, stirring occasionally, until lightly browned, about 2 minutes. Add garlic; cook for 1 minute. Add broth, Slow Cooker Brisket, tomato, beans, chiles, tomato paste, salt, chile powder, and cumin. Bring to a boil; reduce heat to medium-low, and simmer for 20 minutes. Garnish with cheese and jalapeño, if desired. Serve with chips.

MAIN DISH

ON THE MENU

Main Dish	**Easy Sides**	**Leftovers**
Slow Cooker Pork Roast	Quick Turnip Greens Cheese Grits	Mac and Cheese with Pork Roast Loaded Baked Sweet Potatoes

Slow Cooker Pork Roast

The rich and simple flavor of this roast makes it the perfect recipe for adding to leftovers.

MAKES ABOUT 8 SERVINGS

1   **tablespoon firmly packed light brown sugar**
1   **tablespoon kosher salt**
2   **teaspoons ground black pepper**
1   **(4-to 5-pound) pork shoulder**
2   **cups chopped yellow onion**
6   **cloves garlic**
½   **cup white wine vinegar**
1   **cup chicken broth**
2   **bay leaves**

1. In a small bowl, stir together sugar, salt, and pepper; rub mixture over pork.

2. Transfer pork to a 6-quart slow cooker. Add onion and remaining ingredients.

3. Cover and cook on high for 2 hours. Reduce to low; cook for 6 hours more.

Quick Turnip Greens

MAKES ABOUT 4 SERVINGS

4   slices bacon, chopped
1   cup chopped yellow onion
1   clove garlic, minced
8   cups chopped fresh
     turnip greens
4   cups vegetable broth
¼   cup apple cider vinegar
2   tablespoons firmly packed
     light brown sugar

1. In a large saucepan, cook bacon over medium-high heat until crisp, 8 to 10 minutes. Add onion and garlic; cook, stirring occasionally, until tender, about 3 minutes. Add greens, stirring until slightly wilted. Add broth and remaining ingredients; bring to a boil. Reduce heat to medium-low; cover and cook for 15 minutes more.

Cheese Grits

MAKES ABOUT 4 SERVINGS

4   **cups water**
1   **cup quick-cooking grits**
1   **cup shredded Monterey Jack cheese**
½   **cup shredded sharp Cheddar cheese**
¼   **cup heavy whipping cream**
¼   **teaspoon kosher salt**
¼   **teaspoon ground black pepper**
¼   **teaspoon garlic powder**
Garnish: chopped fresh parsley, shredded sharp Cheddar cheese

1. In a large saucepan, bring 4 cups water to a boil over medium-high heat. Gradually whisk in grits. Reduce heat to medium-low; simmer, stirring frequently, until grits are tender, about 5 minutes. Stir in Monterey Jack, Cheddar, cream, salt, pepper, and garlic powder. Serve immediately. Garnish with parsley and cheese, if desired.

Mac and Cheese with Pork Roast

Adding shredded pork roast takes mac and cheese from a delicious side to a hearty supper.

MAKES ABOUT 6 SERVINGS

3 cups whole milk, divided
2 tablespoons all-purpose flour
1½ cups shredded smoked Cheddar cheese
1 cup shredded American cheese
1 teaspoon dry mustard
¼ teaspoon kosher salt
¼ teaspoon ground black pepper
1 (16-ounce) package penne pasta, cooked
3 cups shredded Slow Cooker Pork Roast (recipe on page 45)
Toppings: shredded Slow Cooker Pork Roast, shredded Cheddar cheese, chopped green onion

1. In a large saucepan, bring 2¾ cups milk to a boil over medium-high heat. In a small bowl, whisk together remaining ¼ cup milk and flour until smooth. Gradually add flour mixture to milk mixture in saucepan; whisk until thickened, about 2 minutes. Reduce heat to medium-low; stir in cheeses, mustard, salt, and pepper. Add pasta and pork, stirring to combine.

2. Preheat broiler. Top pasta mixture with additional Slow Cooker Pork Roast and Cheddar. Broil until cheese melts slightly, 1 to 2 minutes. Garnish with green onion, if desired.

Loaded Baked Sweet Potatoes

Who says sweet potatoes have to be sweet? Salsa and jalapeño bring savory south-of-the-border flavor to this main dish.

MAKES ABOUT 4 SERVINGS

4 large sweet potatoes
2 tablespoons vegetable oil
½ teaspoon kosher salt, divided
¼ teaspoon ground black pepper
½ cup sour cream
1 tablespoon chopped fresh jalapeño pepper, seeds removed
1 teaspoon lime zest
1 tablespoon fresh lime juice
2 cups shredded Slow Cooker Pork Roast (recipe on page 45)
1 cup salsa
1 tablespoon chopped fresh cilantro

1. Preheat oven to 400°. Line a rimmed baking sheet with foil. Rub potatoes with oil; sprinkle with ¼ teaspoon salt and pepper. Bake until tender, about 1 hour. Split potatoes; fluff with a fork.

2. In a small bowl, stir together remaining ¼ teaspoon salt, sour cream, jalapeño, and lime zest and juice.

3. Top each potato with ½ cup Slow Cooker Pork Roast, ¼ cup salsa, 2 tablespoons sour cream mixture, and cilantro. Serve immediately.

MAIN DISH

ON THE MENU

Main Dish
Slow Cooker
Turkey Breast

Easy Sides
Cornbread Dressing
Maple-Glazed
Vegetables

Leftovers
Turkey Posole
Turkey Spaghetti

Slow Cooker Turkey Breast

Give yourself a break this Thanksgiving and use your slow cooker to make this tender turkey.

MAKES ABOUT 6 SERVINGS

Turkey:
1   (6- to 7-pound) bone-in,
     skin-on turkey breast
2   tablespoons chopped fresh
     thyme or 2 teaspoons
     dried thyme
1   teaspoon onion powder
½   teaspoon salt
½   teaspoon ground black pepper
1   tablespoon canola oil
1   cup chicken broth

Gravy:
¼   cup all-purpose flour
½   teaspoon ground black pepper
2   cups reserved turkey drippings
Salt, to taste

Garnish: fresh thyme

1. For turkey: Pat turkey dry with paper towels. Using your fingers, gently loosen skin from turkey breast. In a small bowl, stir together thyme, onion powder, salt, and pepper. Rub mixture under skin.

2. In a large skillet, heat oil over medium-high heat. Cook turkey until browned on both sides, about 2 minutes per side. Remove from heat.

3. Place turkey in a 6-quart slow cooker. Add broth to skillet, stirring to loosen browned bits. Add broth mixture to slow cooker. Cover and cook on low until tender, 5 to 6 hours.

4. Remove turkey from slow cooker. Cut into slices; place on a serving platter. Cover with foil. Strain turkey drippings; reserve 2 cups.

5. For gravy: In a medium saucepan, add flour and pepper. Whisk in 2 cups reserved turkey drippings. Bring to a boil over medium-high heat, whisking constantly. Reduce heat to medium-low; simmer until thickened, about 2 minutes. Add salt to taste. Serve gravy with turkey. Garnish with thyme, if desired.

Cornbread Dressing

MAKES ABOUT 10 SERVINGS

1 tablespoon vegetable oil
1 cup chopped yellow onion
1 cup chopped celery
5 cups cubed day-old cornbread
5 cups cubed day-old white bread
3 cups chicken broth
3 tablespoons unsalted butter, melted and divided
3 tablespoons finely chopped fresh sage
3 tablespoons finely chopped fresh parsley
1½ teaspoons salt
¾ teaspoon ground black pepper
2 large eggs, lightly beaten

1. Preheat oven to 350°. Spray a 2½-quart baking dish with cooking spray.

2. In a medium skillet, heat oil over medium-high heat. Add onion and celery; cook until softened, about 5 minutes.

3. In a large bowl, gently stir together onion mixture, breads, broth, 2 tablespoons melted butter, sage, parsley, salt, pepper, and eggs. Spoon into prepared dish. Drizzle with remaining 1 tablespoon melted butter.

4. Bake until lightly browned, about 40 minutes.

Maple-Glazed Vegetables

MAKES ABOUT 8 SERVINGS

1	pound parsnips, peeled and chopped into 2-inch pieces
1	pound carrots, peeled and chopped into 2-inch pieces
¾	pound Brussels sprouts, trimmed and halved
1	medium red onion, peeled and cut into 8 wedges
2	tablespoons canola oil, divided
¾	teaspoon kosher salt
¼	teaspoon ground black pepper
½	cup pure maple syrup, divided
¼	cup water
1	tablespoon fresh thyme
2	tablespoons sherry vinegar
⅓	cup chopped toasted pecans

Garnish: fresh thyme sprigs

1. In a large bowl, toss together parsnips, carrots, Brussels sprouts, red onion, 1 tablespoon oil, salt, and pepper.

2. In a 12-inch cast-iron skillet, heat remaining 1 tablespoon oil over medium-high heat. Add parsnip mixture; cook until lightly browned, about 3 minutes, stirring occasionally. Stir in ¼ cup maple syrup, ¼ cup water, and thyme; cover and reduce heat to medium-low. Cook until tender, about 20 minutes, stirring occasionally.

3. Stir in vinegar and remaining ¼ cup maple syrup. Cook, uncovered, for 5 minutes. Sprinkle with pecans. Garnish with thyme, if desired.

Turkey Posole

If you like chicken tortilla soup, you'll love this flavor-packed version.

MAKES 8 TO 10 SERVINGS

2 tablespoons canola oil

1½ cups chopped yellow onion

3 tablespoons minced fresh garlic

2 carrots, chopped

6 cups turkey or chicken broth

4 cups shredded Slow Cooker Turkey Breast (recipe on page 53)

2 (15-ounce) cans hominy, drained

1 (16-ounce) jar fire-roasted green chile salsa*

1 (10-ounce) can tomatoes with green chiles, undrained

20 stems fresh cilantro, tied together

2 bay leaves

1 tablespoon ground cumin

2 teaspoons dried oregano

¼ teaspoon ground black pepper

1 (4-inch) strip lime zest

Salt, to taste

Garnish: cilantro leaves, sliced radish, lime wedges, queso fresco, sliced avocado

1. In a large skillet, heat oil over medium-high heat. Add onion and garlic; cook, stirring occasionally, until softened, about 6 minutes. Stir in carrot; cook until tender, about 10 minutes. Transfer onion mixture to a 6-quart slow cooker.

2. Stir in broth, turkey, hominy, salsa, tomatoes, cilantro, bay leaves, cumin, oregano, pepper, and zest.

3. Cover and cook on low for 6 to 7 hours. Remove and discard cilantro and zest. Season with salt, if desired. Garnish with cilantro, radish, lime wedges, queso fresco, and avocado, if desired.

*We used Hatch.

Turkey Spaghetti

Topped with Cheddar, this hearty supper is the comfort food
we crave and makes the most of your leftover turkey.

MAKES ABOUT 6 SERVINGS

¼ cup unsalted butter
½ cup chopped yellow onion
1 cup chopped green bell pepper
1 cup chopped red bell pepper
1 clove garlic, minced
3 tablespoons all-purpose flour
2 cups chicken broth
1 cup half-and-half
½ cup grated Parmesan cheese
4 cups chopped Slow Cooker Turkey Breast (recipe on page 53)
½ (16-ounce) package spaghetti, cooked according to package directions
½ cup shredded sharp Cheddar cheese

1. Preheat oven 350°.
2. In a 10-inch cast-iron skillet, melt butter over medium heat. Add onion, bell peppers, and garlic. Cook, stirring occasionally, until vegetables are tender, about 5 minutes. Stir in flour; cook for 1 to 2 minutes. Add broth; cook, stirring frequently, until bubbly, 3 to 4 minutes. Whisk in half-and-half; cook, stirring constantly, until bubbly. Stir in Parmesan; remove from heat. Stir in turkey and cooked pasta.
3. Bake until bubbly, 15 to 20 minutes. Sprinkle with Cheddar, and bake until cheese melts, 3 to 4 minutes more. Let stand for 5 minutes before serving.

KITCHEN TIP

To get a head start on this easy skillet supper, chop the vegetables the night before.

Soups & Breads

ON A BUSY NIGHT, NOTHING IS MORE WELCOMING THAN A HOT
BOWL OF SOUP AND HOMEMADE BREAD FOR SUPPER

Chicken and Wild Rice Soup

Wild rice and creamy broth make this soup the perfect rainy-day meal.

MAKES 6 TO 8 SERVINGS

2 tablespoons canola oil

2 bone-in, skinless chicken breasts

3 teaspoons kosher salt, divided

¾ teaspoon ground black pepper, divided

8 cups low-sodium chicken broth

2 cups chopped yellow onion

1 cup matchstick carrots

1 cup wild rice

2 teaspoons minced fresh garlic

1 small bunch fresh thyme, tied with kitchen twine

1 tablespoon red wine vinegar

½ cup heavy whipping cream

Garnish: chopped fresh parsley

1. In a large skillet, heat oil over medium-high heat. Sprinkle chicken with 1 teaspoon salt and ½ teaspoon pepper. Cook chicken until browned, 3 to 4 minutes per side. Place chicken in a 5- to 6-quart slow cooker.

2. Add remaining 2 teaspoons salt, remaining ¼ teaspoon pepper, broth, onion, carrot, rice, garlic, thyme, and vinegar to slow cooker.

3. Cover and cook on low for 6 hours or until chicken is cooked through, or on high for 4 hours. Remove thyme; discard. Remove chicken from slow cooker. Shred meat; discard bones. Return chicken to slow cooker. Stir in cream. Garnish with parsley, if desired.

Braised Pork Stew

Sausage and fire-roasted tomatoes take this stew to the next level.

MAKES 8 TO 10 SERVINGS

3   **pounds boneless pork shoulder**
1½ **teaspoons kosher salt, divided**
1   **teaspoon ground black pepper, divided**
2   **tablespoons canola oil**
1   **pound smoked sausage, cut into 1-inch pieces**
2   **cups chopped yellow onion**
1   **cup chopped carrot**
½   **cup chopped celery**
2   **cloves garlic**
¼   **cup tomato paste**
1   **(14.5-ounce) can diced fire-roasted tomatoes, drained**
3   **(15.5-ounce) cans cannellini beans, drained and rinsed**
1¼ **cups chicken broth**
2   **tablespoons chopped fresh rosemary**
½   **cup chopped fresh parsley**
2   **tablespoons red wine vinegar**
1   **cup panko (Japanese bread crumbs)**
2   **tablespoons butter, melted**

1. Trim excess fat from pork shoulder; cut into 1-inch pieces. Sprinkle with 1 teaspoon salt and ½ teaspoon pepper.

2. In a large skillet, heat oil over medium-high heat. Working in batches, cook pork until browned, about 3 minutes. Remove from pan with a slotted spoon. Add sausage, onion, carrot, and celery to pan; cook until lightly browned, about 3 minutes. Add garlic; cook for 1 minute more.

3. In a 5- to 6-quart slow cooker, combine pork shoulder, sausage mixture, tomato paste, tomatoes, beans, broth, rosemary, remaining ½ teaspoon salt, and remaining ½ teaspoon pepper.

4. Cover and cook on low for 8 hours or until tender, or on high for 4 hours. Let stand for 15 minutes; skim excess fat. Stir in parsley and vinegar.

5. Preheat oven to 350°. On a small rimmed baking sheet, toss together breadcrumbs and melted butter. Bake until lightly toasted, about 7 minutes, stirring once. Sprinkle servings with bread crumbs.

Ham, Bean, and Collard Greens Soup

Make the most of winter's harvest with this soup.

MAKES ABOUT 6 SERVINGS

2 (15.5-ounce) cans cannellini beans, drained and rinsed
4 cups chicken broth
4 cups chopped fresh collard greens
2 cups water
1½ cups sliced parsnip
1½ cups chopped peeled sweet potato
1½ cups chopped ham
1 cup chopped yellow onion
2 tablespoons chopped fresh sage
1½ teaspoons kosher salt
½ teaspoon crushed red pepper
2 smoked ham hocks
2 tablespoons distilled white vinegar
Garnish: grated Parmesan cheese

1. In a medium bowl, mash 1 can of beans; reserve mashed beans.

2. In a 5- to 6-quart slow cooker, combine remaining can of cannellini beans, broth, greens, water, parsnip, sweet potato, ham, onion, sage, salt, crushed red pepper, and ham hocks.

3. Cover and cook on low for 7 hours or until tender, or on high for 4 hours. Remove ham hocks. Stir in reserved mashed beans and vinegar. Garnish servings with cheese, if desired.

Chicken Tortilla Soup

This soup is full of Southwestern flavor thanks to fire-roasted tomatoes and cumin.

MAKES ABOUT 10 SERVINGS

1 tablespoon canola oil
3 boneless skinless chicken breasts (about 2¼ pounds)
3½ teaspoons kosher salt, divided
½ teaspoon ground black pepper
8 cups low-sodium chicken broth
2 cups chopped yellow onion
1 tablespoon minced fresh garlic
1 (14.5-ounce) can diced fire-roasted tomatoes
2 teaspoons ground cumin
1 teaspoon dried oregano
½ teaspoon smoked paprika
2 (14.5-ounce) cans black beans, drained and rinsed
Garnish: tortilla chips, cilantro, lime wedges, shredded Cheddar cheese, sliced jalapeño pepper

1. In a large skillet, heat oil over medium-high heat. Sprinkle chicken with 1 teaspoon salt and pepper. Cook chicken until browned on both sides, 3 to 4 minutes per side. Place chicken in a 5- to 6-quart slow cooker.

2. Add remaining 2½ teaspoons salt, broth, onion, garlic, tomatoes, cumin, oregano, and paprika to slow cooker.

3. Cover and cook on low for 6 hours or until cooked through, or on high for 4 hours. Shred chicken; stir in beans, and cook for 30 minutes more. Garnish servings with chips, cilantro, lime, cheese, and jalapeño, if desired.

Loaded Baked Potato Soup

Topped with bacon and cheese, potato soup has never tasted so good.

MAKES ABOUT 6 SERVINGS

3 pounds baking potatoes, peeled and cut into 1-inch cubes
3 cups chicken broth
2 cups water, divided
½ cup chopped yellow onion
2 teaspoons kosher salt
½ teaspoon ground black pepper
½ teaspoon garlic powder
1 cup heavy whipping cream, warmed
Garnish: crumbled cooked bacon, chopped fresh dill, shredded Cheddar cheese, ground black pepper

1. In a 5- to 6-quart slow cooker, combine potatoes, broth, 1½ cups water, onion, salt, pepper, and garlic powder.

2. Cover and cook on low for 9 hours or until potatoes are tender, or on high for 5 hours. Using a potato masher, mash to desired consistency. Stir in cream and remaining ½ cup water, if needed. Garnish servings with bacon, dill, cheese, and pepper, if desired.

Collard Greens and Smoked Sausage Stew

Tomatoes and vinegar punch up the flavor of this hearty stew.

MAKES 6 TO 8 SERVINGS

1 (1-pound) package smoked sausage, thinly sliced
2 cups chopped yellow onion
1 cup chopped green bell pepper
1 tablespoon minced fresh garlic
4 cups chopped collard greens, stems removed
1 (28-ounce) can plum tomatoes, drained and crushed
6 cups low-sodium chicken broth
2½ teaspoons kosher salt
2 teaspoons sugar
¼ teaspoon ground black pepper
2 teaspoons apple cider vinegar
1 teaspoon hot sauce

1. Heat a large nonstick skillet over medium-high heat. Add sausage, onion, pepper, and garlic to skillet. Cook, stirring frequently, until sausage is browned and vegetables are tender, about 6 minutes. Transfer sausage mixture to a 5- to 6-quart slow cooker. Add collards, tomatoes, broth, salt, sugar, and pepper.

2. Cover and cook on low for 6 hours, or on high for 4 hours. Stir in vinegar and hot sauce just before serving.

Chicken and Black-Eyed Pea Stew

This stew is perfect for New Year's Day or any winter day.

MAKES 6 TO 8 SERVINGS

1 tablespoon canola oil
1½ cups chopped yellow onion
½ cup chopped carrot
½ cup chopped celery
2 cloves garlic, minced
4 cups shredded cooked chicken
4 (15.5-ounce) cans black-eyed peas, drained and rinsed
1 (14.5-ounce) can fire-roasted tomatoes, drained
4 cups chicken broth
4 sprigs fresh thyme
2 bay leaves
2 teaspoons smoked paprika
1 teaspoon kosher salt
½ teaspoon ground black pepper
¼ teaspoon crushed red pepper
2 tablespoons apple cider vinegar
Garnish: chopped green onion, chopped fresh thyme, ground black pepper

1. In a medium skillet, heat oil over medium-high heat. Add onion, carrot, and celery; cook, stirring occasionally, until lightly browned, about 3 minutes. Add garlic; cook for 1 minute more.

2. In a 5- to 6-quart slow cooker, combine onion mixture, chicken, peas, tomatoes, broth, thyme, bay leaves, paprika, salt, and peppers.

3. Cover and cook on low for 7 hours or until vegetables are tender, or on high for 4 hours. Discard thyme and bay leaves. Stir in vinegar. Garnish servings with green onion, thyme, and pepper, if desired.

Vegetable Beef Soup

Add your favorite in-season vegetables for a twist on this hearty and comforting classic.

MAKES 6 TO 8 SERVINGS

3 tablespoons canola oil
2 pounds top round steak, cut into ¾-inch pieces
2½ teaspoons kosher salt, divided
1 teaspoon ground black pepper, divided
1½ cups chopped yellow onion
1½ cups chopped carrot
½ cup chopped celery
2 cloves garlic, minced
5 cups beef broth
4 sprigs fresh thyme
2 cups chopped peeled baking potatoes
1 cup sliced fresh green beans
1 (14.5-ounce) can diced fire-roasted tomatoes, undrained
2 tablespoons tomato paste
2 tablespoons chopped fresh parsley
1 tablespoon red wine vinegar

1. In a large skillet, heat oil over medium-high heat. Sprinkle beef with 1 teaspoon salt and ½ teaspoon pepper. Working in batches, cook beef, stirring occasionally, until browned, about 3 minutes. Set aside. Add onion, carrot, and celery to pan; cook until lightly browned, about 3 minutes. Add garlic; cook for 1 minute more.

2. In a 5- to 6-quart slow cooker, combine beef, onion mixture, broth, thyme, potatoes, green beans, tomatoes, tomato paste, remaining 1½ teaspoons salt and remaining ½ teaspoon pepper.

3. Cover and cook on low for 7 hours or until tender, or on high for 4 hours. Discard thyme. Stir in parsley and vinegar.

Slow Cooker Sausage and Seafood Gumbo

Craving the flavors of to the Big Easy? This gumbo delivers.

MAKES 8 TO 10 SERVINGS

1 pound smoked sausage, sliced
½ cup vegetable oil
¾ cup all-purpose flour
2 cups chopped yellow onion
2 cups chopped celery
1 cup chopped green bell pepper
1 tablespoon minced fresh garlic (about 4 cloves)
1 jalapeño pepper, minced
4 cups chicken broth
2 tablespoons chopped fresh thyme, divided
1 teaspoon salt
½ teaspoon ground black pepper
4 bay leaves
1 (14.5-ounce) can fire-roasted tomatoes, undrained
2 pounds medium fresh shrimp, peeled and deveined, tails left on
¾ pound fresh steamed crab claws
1 teaspoon Creole seasoning
Cooked rice, to serve
Garnish: sliced green onion

1. In a 12-inch cast-iron skillet, cook sausage over medium heat, stirring occasionally, until browned, about 7 minutes. Remove sausage from skillet. Set aside. Discard rendered fat in skillet.

2. Carefully wipe skillet. Add oil; heat over medium heat. Add flour, stirring until smooth. Cook, stirring constantly with a wooden spoon, until mixture is a deep caramel color, about 30 minutes. Add onion, celery, bell pepper, garlic, and jalapeño; cook, stirring constantly, until softened, about 5 minutes.

3. Gradually stir in broth. Bring to a boil; reduce heat to medium-low. Simmer, stirring constantly, until mixture is smooth and has thickened, about 2 minutes. Transfer to a 5- to 6-quart slow cooker. Add sausage, 1 tablespoon thyme, salt, pepper, bay leaves, and tomatoes.

4. Cover and cook on low for 5 hours. Add shrimp, crab claws, Creole seasoning, and remaining 1 tablespoon thyme. Cover, and cook on high until shrimp are pink and firm, about 30 minutes, stirring twice. Discard bay leaves. Serve over rice. Garnish with green onion, if desired.

Chicken Noodle Soup

Cozy and comforting, this soup is the perfect cure for whatever ails you.

MAKES ABOUT 10 SERVINGS

4 cups shredded cooked chicken
8 cups chicken broth
1 cup water
1 cup sliced carrot
1 cup chopped yellow onion
½ cup chopped celery
1½ teaspoons kosher salt
½ teaspoon ground black pepper
4 sprigs fresh thyme
½ pound medium egg noodles, cooked
2 tablespoons fresh lemon juice
Garnish: fresh thyme, ground black pepper

1. In a 5- to 6-quart slow cooker, combine chicken, broth, 1 cup water, carrot, onion, celery, salt, pepper, and thyme.
2. Cover and cook on high for 4 hours or until vegetables are tender, or on low for 7 hours. Discard thyme sprigs. Stir in noodles and lemon juice. Garnish servings with thyme and pepper, if desired.

Southern Minestrone

An Italian classic gets a Southern makeover with the addition of field peas and pinto beans.

MAKES 8 TO 10 SERVINGS

1¼ pounds ground mild Italian pork sausage
2 cups chopped yellow onion
1 cup chopped carrot
1 cup chopped celery
2 teaspoons minced fresh garlic
6 cups vegetable broth
2 (16-ounce) cans pinto beans, drained and rinsed
1 (14.5-ounce) can diced tomatoes, undrained
1 cup fresh or frozen field peas with snaps
1¼ teaspoons salt
1 teaspoon ground black pepper
½ teaspoon ground oregano
2 cups dried pasta, such as ditalini
2 tablespoons red wine vinegar
Garnish: fresh parsley, Parmesan cheese

1. In a medium skillet, cook sausage over medium heat until browned. Drain, if necessary.

2. In a 5- to 6-quart slow cooker, add cooked sausage, onion, carrot, celery, garlic, broth, beans, tomatoes, peas, salt, pepper, and oregano. Cover and cook on low for 6 hours.

3. During the last 30 minutes of cooking, add pasta and vinegar. Cook, uncovered, until pasta is tender. Garnish with parsley and cheese, if desired.

Bacon-Cheddar Buttermilk Biscuits

If you thought buttermilk biscuits couldn't get better, try these with cheese and bacon.

MAKES 8

2   cups all-purpose flour
2   tablespoons sugar
1   tablespoon baking powder
1   teaspoon kosher salt
½   teaspoon baking soda
7   tablespoons cold unsalted butter, cubed
1   cup shredded Cheddar cheese, divided
½   cup chopped cooked bacon, divided
¼   cup finely chopped green onion
1   cup plus 2 tablespoons cold whole buttermilk, divided

1. Line a 5- to 6-quart slow cooker with parchment paper.
2. In a medium bowl, whisk together flour, sugar, baking powder, salt, and baking soda. Using a pastry blender or 2 forks, cut in butter until mixture is crumbly. Stir in ½ cup cheese, ¼ cup bacon, and green onion. Gradually add 1 cup buttermilk, stirring just until dry ingredients are moistened.
3. On a lightly floured surface, gently pat dough into a rectangle, and fold into thirds; repeat twice. Roll dough ¾ inch thick. Using a 2½-inch round cutter, cut dough, rerolling scraps once. Place biscuits in slow cooker; brush with remaining 2 tablespoons buttermilk, and sprinkle with remaining ½ cup cheese and remaining ¼ cup bacon.
4. Cover and cook on high until edges are golden and tops are set, 1½ to 2 hours. Using parchment as handles, remove biscuits from slow cooker.

Honey-Oat Wheat Bread

Serve this hearty bread at dinner, or use it to make sandwiches.

MAKES 1 LOAF

½   cup old-fashioned oats
¼   cup honey
2   tablespoons unsalted butter, softened
2   teaspoons kosher salt
½   teaspoon ground cinnamon
1   cup water
¼   cup whole milk
2   teaspoons active dry yeast
2   cups all-purpose flour
1   cup whole wheat flour
Garnish: old-fashioned oats, sesame seeds, sunflower seeds, poppy seeds, kosher salt

1. In the bowl of a stand mixer fitted with the dough hook attachment, combine oats, honey, butter, salt, and cinnamon.

2. In a small saucepan, bring 1 cup water and milk to a boil over medium heat. Pour over oat mixture, stirring to combine. Let cool for 15 to 20 minutes.

3. Add yeast, and let stand for 1 minute. Add flours, and beat at medium speed until smooth and elastic, about 5 minutes, stopping to scrape sides of bowl.

4. Turn out dough onto a lightly floured surface, and knead 5 times. Shape dough into a ball, and cover with plastic wrap. Let rest for 15 minutes.

5. Punch dough down, and shape into a ball. Line a 5- to 6-quart slow cooker with parchment paper. Place dough in slow cooker, and garnish as desired.

6. Cover and cook on high until an instant-read thermometer inserted in thickest portion registers 200°, about 2½ hours. Let cool completely on a wire rack.

Southwestern Cornbread

Thought cornbread had to be made in a skillet? Think again.

MAKES 8 SERVINGS

1½ cups all-purpose flour
1½ cups plain yellow cornmeal
¼ cup sugar
4 teaspoons baking powder
1 teaspoon kosher salt
½ teaspoon ground red pepper
2 large eggs, lightly beaten
2 cups whole buttermilk
1 (4.5-ounce) can chopped green chiles, drained
1 cup shredded Cheddar cheese, divided
½ cup diced tomatoes
¼ cup diced yellow onion
Garnish: sliced green onion

1. Line a 5- to 6-quart slow cooker with parchment paper.

2. In a medium bowl, whisk together flour, cornmeal, sugar, baking powder, salt, and red pepper. Add eggs, buttermilk, chiles, ½ cup cheese, tomatoes, and onion; stir just until dry ingredients are moistened. Pour mixture into slow cooker. Top with remaining ½ cup cheese.

3. Cover and cook on high until a wooden pick inserted in center comes out clean, about 2 hours. Transfer slow cooker insert to a wire rack to let cool slightly. Using parchment as handles, remove from slow cooker, and cut into 8 wedges. Garnish with green onion, if desired.

Pull-Apart Garlic-Cheddar Knots

Store-bought pizza dough makes these pull-apart knots come together in a flash.

MAKES 24

3 tablespoons olive oil
2 tablespoons unsalted butter
3 tablespoons minced garlic
¼ teaspoon crushed red pepper
¼ cup chopped fresh rosemary
1 (16-ounce) bag pizza dough
1 cup finely shredded smoked
   Cheddar cheese
Marinara sauce, to serve

1. Line a 5- to 6-quart slow cooker with parchment paper.
2. In a small skillet, heat oil and butter over medium heat until butter is melted and bubbling. Add garlic and red pepper; cook until fragrant, about 1 minute. Remove from heat, and stir in rosemary. Transfer to a large bowl.
3. On a lightly floured surface, divide pizza dough into 2 equal pieces. Roll each piece into an 8x4-inch rectangle. Cut each rectangle into 12 (4-inch) strips. Tie each strip into a knot, and toss in garlic mixture. Place knots in slow cooker in an even layer.
4. Cover and cook on high for 1 hour and 15 minutes. Sprinkle with cheese; cover and cook until edges are golden brown, about 30 minutes more. Using parchment as handles, remove rolls from slow cooker. Serve with marinara sauce.

Corn Spoonbread

This moist and flavorful side is a cross between soufflé and cornbread.

MAKES ABOUT 8 SERVINGS

½ cup plain yellow cornmeal
½ cup all-purpose flour
4 teaspoons baking powder
2 teaspoons kosher salt
1 (8-ounce) package cream cheese, softened
½ cup sugar
2 large eggs
2 tablespoons unsalted butter, melted
1 cup whole milk
1 (16-ounce) can cut corn kernels, drained and rinsed
1 (14-ounce) can cream-style corn
Garnish: crumbled cooked bacon, Buttermilk Whipped Cream (recipe follows)

1. Spray a 6-quart slow cooker with baking spray with flour.
2. In a small bowl, whisk together cornmeal, flour, baking powder, and salt.
3. In the bowl of a stand mixer, beat cream cheese and sugar at medium speed until smooth. Add eggs and melted butter, and beat until combined. Gradually beat in milk until combined. Stir in corn and cream-style corn. Stir in cornmeal mixture just until combined. Pour into slow cooker.
4. Cover and cook on high until center is almost set, 2 to 2½ hours. Transfer slow cooker insert to a wire rack to let cool slightly. Garnish servings with bacon and Buttermilk Whipped Cream, if desired.

Buttermilk Whipped Cream

MAKES ABOUT 3 CUPS

1 cup heavy whipping cream
½ cup whole buttermilk
3 tablespoons confectioners' sugar
1½ teaspoons kosher salt

1. In a large bowl, beat cream, buttermilk, confectioners' sugar, and salt with a mixer at medium speed until soft peaks form.

Desserts

TRANSFORM YOUR SLOW COOKER INTO A COUNTERTOP OVEN
TO MAKE THESE DELICIOUS CANDIES, CAKES, AND COBBLERS
FOR YOUR FRIENDS AND FAMILY

Mississippi Mud Fudge

Pecans add the perfect crunch to this simple fudge.

MAKES ABOUT 12 SERVINGS

2   cups semisweet chocolate morsels
1   (14-ounce) can sweetened condensed milk
½   cup unsalted butter
½   cup heavy whipping cream
⅓   cup light corn syrup
1   teaspoon vanilla extract
¼   teaspoon salt
1   cup chopped pecans, toasted
2   cups miniature marshmallows

1. Spray an 8x8-inch baking pan with cooking spray. Line bottom of pan with parchment paper, letting ends extend over sides of pan.

2. Spray the insert of a 4-quart slow cooker with cooking spray; add chocolate morsels, condensed milk, butter, cream, corn syrup, vanilla, and salt, stirring to combine.

3. Cover and cook on low for 1 hour, stirring every 15 minutes. Pour mixture into prepared pan. Sprinkle with pecans and marshmallows, pressing gently. Let cool completely, about 2 hours. Using parchment as handles, remove fudge from pan; cut into squares. Store in an airtight container at room temperature for up to 3 days.

White Chocolate-Almond Drop Candy

These salty-sweet treats make a delicious gift during the holidays.

MAKES ABOUT 40

1 pound vanilla-flavored candy coating, chopped

2½ cups white chocolate morsels*

3 cups coarsely crushed pretzel sticks

½ cup slivered almonds, toasted

1. Line several large baking sheets with parchment paper.

2. Spray the insert of a 5- to 6-quart slow cooker with cooking spray. Add candy coating and white chocolate morsels, spreading in an even layer.

3. Cover and cook on low until coating and morsels begin to melt, about 1 hour. Whisk mixture until almost smooth. Stir in pretzels and almonds. Turn slow cooker off. Drop candy by tablespoonfuls onto prepared baking pans. Let stand until set, about 2 hours.

We used Ghirardelli.

Candied Pecans

Orange zest wakes up these pecans with a little zing of flavor.

MAKES 6 CUPS

6　cups pecan halves
1　cup granulated sugar
1　cup firmly packed light
　　brown sugar
2　tablespoons ground cinnamon
1½　teaspoons ground cardamom
1　teaspoon salt
3　large egg whites
2　teaspoons vanilla extract
1　teaspoon orange zest
½　cup water

1. Spray the insert of a 4-quart slow cooker with cooking spray; add pecans.

2. In a medium bowl, combine sugars, cinnamon, cardamom, and salt. In a small bowl, whisk together egg whites, vanilla, and zest until frothy. Add egg white mixture to pecans, stirring until combined. Stir in sugar mixture.

3. Cover and cook on low for 2½ hours, stirring every 30 minutes. Stir in ½ cup water until combined.

4. Cover and cook on high for 15 to 30 minutes, stirring occasionally.

5. Line 2 baking sheets with parchment paper. Spread pecans on prepared pans in an even layer. Let cool completely. Store in an airtight container for up to 2 weeks.

Butterscotch Pecan Fudge

Studded with toasted pecans, this fudge is irresistible.

MAKES ABOUT 16 SERVINGS

3   cups butterscotch morsels
1   (14-ounce) can sweetened condensed milk
½   cup chopped vanilla-flavored candy coating
1   tablespoon unsalted butter, diced
2½ cups toasted pecans, chopped
1   teaspoon vanilla extract

1. Line an 8-inch square baking pan with foil, letting excess extend over sides of pan. Spray foil with cooking spray.
2. Spray the insert of a 5- to 6-quart slow cooker with cooking spray. Add butterscotch morsels, condensed milk, candy coating, and butter.
3. Cover and cook on low until mixture begins to melt, about 1 hour. Whisk until smooth. Stir in pecans and vanilla. Spread evenly into prepared pan. Cover and refrigerate until firm, about 6 hours.
4. Let stand until slightly softened, about 20 minutes. Using foil as handles, remove from pan. Cut into squares. Cover and refrigerate for up to 2 weeks.

Cranberry-Apple Crisp

This crisp is the perfect marriage between two fall favorites—apples and cranberries.

MAKES 8 TO 10 SERVINGS

4 cups chopped peeled Granny Smith apples

3 cups fresh or frozen whole cranberries

1½ cups granulated sugar

¾ cup all-purpose flour, divided

1½ cups old-fashioned oats

1 cup chopped pecans

½ cup firmly packed light brown sugar

½ cup unsalted butter, melted

1½ teaspoons pumpkin pie spice

Vanilla ice cream, to serve

Garnish: chopped toasted pecans

1. Spray a 5- to 6-quart slow cooker with cooking spray.

2. In a large bowl, combine apples, cranberries, granulated sugar, and ¼ cup flour. Pour into slow cooker.

3. In a medium bowl, combine oats, pecans, brown sugar, melted butter, pumpkin pie spice, and remaining ½ cup flour. Sprinkle over apple mixture.

4. Cover and cook on high until filling is bubbly, about 2½ hours. Let cool slightly before serving. Serve with vanilla ice cream. Garnish with pecans, if desired.

Espresso Lava Cake

Add a dollop of ice cream to this cake and you've got heaven in a bowl.

MAKES 8 TO 10 SERVINGS

1 (15.25-ounce) box German chocolate cake mix*
1¼ cups whole milk
½ cup vegetable oil
3 large eggs, at room temperature
3 tablespoons instant coffee, divided
1¼ cups boiling water
½ cup sugar
3 tablespoons unsweetened cocoa powder
¼ teaspoon salt
1 cup mini semisweet chocolate morsels
1 cup chocolate chunks
Chocolate ice cream, to serve
Garnish: chocolate-covered espresso beans

1. Spray a 5- to 6-quart slow cooker with baking spray with flour.

2. In a large bowl, beat cake mix, milk, oil, eggs, and 2 tablespoons coffee with a mixer at medium speed until combined, about 2 minutes. Pour into slow cooker.

3. In a medium bowl, stir together 1¼ cups boiling water, sugar, cocoa, salt, and remaining 1 tablespoon coffee. Gently pour over batter. (Do not mix.) Sprinkle chocolate morsels over batter in slow cooker.

4. Cover and cook on high for 2 hours. Uncover and sprinkle with chocolate chunks. Cover and let stand on warm for 5 minutes. Spoon into bowls while still warm. Serve with chocolate ice cream. Garnish with chocolate-covered espresso beans, if desired.

*We used Duncan Hines.

Chocolate-Hazelnut Cake

With its gorgeous swirls, you'd never guess this cake came out of a slow cooker.

MAKES 8 TO 10 SERVINGS

Cake:
1   (15.25-ounce) box yellow cake mix*
1   cup water
⅓   cup vegetable oil
4   large eggs
3   tablespoons chocolate-hazelnut spread*

Frosting:
½   cup unsalted butter, softened
2   cups confectioners' sugar
½   cup unsweetened cocoa powder
¼   cup chocolate-hazelnut spread*
2½ tablespoons heavy whipping cream

Garnish: chopped hazelnuts

1. Spray a 5- to 6-quart slow cooker with baking spray with flour.
2. For cake: In a large bowl, beat cake mix, 1 cup water, oil, and eggs with a mixer at medium speed until combined, about 2 minutes. Place one-third of batter in a medium bowl; stir in chocolate-hazelnut spread.
3. Pour one-third of plain cake batter into slow cooker. Top with chocolate-hazelnut batter; add remaining plain cake batter. Swirl batters together gently with a spatula.
4. Cover and cook on high until a wooden pick inserted in center comes out clean, about 2 hours. Remove slow cooker insert, and let cool on a wire rack. Loosen edges of cake from sides with a knife or spatula. Turn out cake onto a serving plate.
5. For frosting: In a large bowl, beat butter with a mixer at medium speed until creamy, about 2 minutes. Gradually add confectioners' sugar, beating until smooth. Add cocoa, chocolate-hazelnut spread, and cream; beat until combined. Increase mixer speed to medium, and beat until fluffy. Spread frosting on top and sides of cake. Garnish with hazelnuts, if desired.

*We used Duncan Hines and Nutella.

Apple Cobbler

Sweet, tender apples pair perfectly with buttermilk biscuits drenched in caramel sauce.

MAKES 8 SERVINGS

5   Honey Crisp apples, cored and
     sliced into 8 sections
½   cup plus 2 tablespoons
     sugar, divided
3   tablespoons cornstarch
2   tablespoons orange zest
2   tablespoons fresh orange juice
3½   teaspoons ground cinnamon,
     divided
½   (10.2-ounce) can refrigerated
     buttermilk biscuits*
Vanilla ice cream and caramel
     sauce, to serve

1. Line a 5- to 6-quart slow cooker with foil.
2. In a large bowl, stir together apples, ½ cup sugar, cornstarch, orange zest and juice, and 2 teaspoons cinnamon until combined. Spoon mixture into slow cooker.
3. Cut biscuits into 6 wedges. Place wedges on top of apples. In a small bowl, combine remaining 2 tablespoons sugar and remaining 1½ teaspoons cinnamon. Sprinkle over biscuit wedges. Cover and cook on high for 2½ hours. Serve with vanilla ice cream and caramel sauce.

We used Pillsbury.

Turtle Brownies

There's no better dessert combination than pecans, caramel, and chocolate.

MAKES 8 TO 10 SERVINGS

2 (4-ounce) bars bittersweet chocolate, chopped
½ cup unsalted butter
1 cup sugar
3 large eggs
1¼ cups all-purpose flour
¼ cup unsweetened cocoa powder
1 teaspoon baking powder
2 teaspoons kosher salt, divided
1 cup semisweet chocolate morsels, divided
1 cup pecans, chopped and divided
25 vanilla caramels, unwrapped
3 tablespoons whole milk

1. Line a 6-quart slow cooker with parchment paper.

2. In a medium microwave-safe bowl, combine chopped chocolate and butter. Microwave on high in 30-second intervals, stirring between each, until chocolate is melted and smooth. Add sugar, whisking to combine. Whisk in eggs.

3. In a medium bowl, whisk together flour, cocoa, baking powder, and 1 teaspoon salt. Add flour mixture to chocolate mixture, stirring just until moistened. Pour mixture into slow cooker. Cover and cook on low until edges are set, 2½ to 3 hours.

4. Transfer slow cooker insert to a wire rack. Sprinkle with ¾ cup chocolate morsels and ¾ cup pecans.

5. In a small saucepan, cook caramels, milk, and remaining 1 teaspoon salt over medium-high heat. Stir until caramels are melted. Drizzle over brownies, and sprinkle with remaining ¼ cup chocolate morsels and remaining ¼ cup pecans. Let cool completely. Using parchment as handles, remove from slow cooker, and cut as desired.

Maple-Pecan Monkey Bread

Feel free to have this dessert for breakfast. We won't tell!

MAKES 8 TO 10 SERVINGS

8　tablespoons unsalted butter, melted and divided

2　tablespoons pure maple syrup

½　cup granulated sugar

¼　cup firmly packed light brown sugar

1　tablespoon apple pie spice

Pinch kosher salt

2　(10.2-ounce) cans refrigerated biscuits*

⅓　cup chopped pecans

1　cup confectioners' sugar, sifted

1½　teaspoons maple extract

1. Spray a 4-quart slow cooker with cooking spray.

2. In a large bowl, combine 4 tablespoons melted butter and maple syrup. In another large bowl, whisk together sugars, apple pie spice, and salt.

3. Cut each biscuit into 6 pieces. Working in batches, dip biscuit pieces in butter mixture, tossing to coat. Place in sugar mixture, tossing to coat.

4. Sprinkle half of pecans in slow cooker. Place one layer of coated biscuit pieces in slow cooker, and sprinkle with remaining pecans. Top with remaining biscuit pieces.

5. Cover and cook on low for 2 to 2½ hours. Let stand for 5 minutes; carefully remove insert and invert onto a serving plate.

6. In a small bowl, whisk together confectioners' sugar, maple extract, and remaining 4 tablespoons melted butter. Drizzle glaze over bread, and serve warm.

*We used Pillsbury.

Bourbon-Raisin Bread Pudding

Drizzled with white chocolate, this bread pudding is a decadent dessert.

MAKES ABOUT 8 SERVINGS

Bread pudding:

1	**cup sugar**
1	**cup whole milk, at room temperature**
½	**cup chopped pecans**
¼	**cup golden raisins**
¼	**cup raisins**
¼	**cup unsalted butter, melted and cooled**
4	**large eggs, room temperature**
2	**teaspoons vanilla extract**
1	**teaspoon ground cinnamon**
1	**(16-ounce) loaf day-old French bread, cubed**

Glaze:

2	**cups white chocolate morsels**
1½	**cups heavy whipping cream**
¼	**cup bourbon**
1½	**teaspoons vanilla extract**

1. Spray a 5- to 6-quart slow cooker with baking spray with flour.

2. For bread pudding: In a large bowl, whisk together sugar, milk, pecans, raisins, melted butter, eggs, vanilla, and cinnamon. Press bread into milk mixture. Let stand for 10 minutes. Add to slow cooker.

3. Cover and cook on low until center is set, 2½ to 3 hours. Let stand for 30 minutes.

4. For glaze: Place white chocolate morsels in a medium bowl. In a medium saucepan, bring cream, bourbon, and vanilla to a boil over medium heat. Pour hot cream mixture over chocolate, stirring until melted. Serve with bread pudding.

Pound Cake with Berry Topping

Use your favorite berries to grace this buttery pound cake.

MAKES 8 TO 10 SERVINGS

Cake:
1½ cups unsalted butter, softened
3   cups sugar
6   large eggs, at room temperature
3   cups all-purpose flour
⅛   teaspoon baking soda
1   (8-ounce) container sour cream, at room temperature

Berry topping:
1   (16-ounce) container fresh strawberries, quartered
1   (6-ounce) container fresh blackberries
1   (6-ounce) container fresh raspberries
¼   cup sugar
1   orange, zested and juiced

1. Line a 5- to 6-quart slow cooker with foil, and line bottom with parchment paper. Spray with cooking spray.

2. For cake: In a large bowl, beat butter and sugar with a mixer at medium speed until fluffy, 3 to 4 minutes, stopping to scrape sides of bowl. Add eggs, one at a time, beating well after each addition.

3. In a medium bowl, whisk together flour and baking soda. Gradually add flour mixture to butter mixture alternately with sour cream, beginning and ending with flour mixture, beating just until combined after each addition. Pour batter into slow cooker.

4. Cover and cook on high until a wooden pick inserted in center comes out clean, 3½ to 4 hours. Let cool for at least 2 hours or overnight.

5. For berry topping: In a large bowl, combine strawberries, blackberries, raspberries, sugar, and orange zest and juice. Let stand for 10 minutes. Using parchment as handles, remove cake from slow cooker. Serve with berry mixture.

Cinnamon Rolls

If you've never had baked-from-scratch cinnamon rolls, let us introduce you to your new favorite breakfast.

MAKES 12

Dough:
1 cup plus 2 tablespoons warm whole milk (120°)
2 teaspoons honey
1 (0.25-ounce) package instant dry yeast
3¼ cups all-purpose flour
¼ cup sugar
½ teaspoon kosher salt
6 tablespoons unsalted butter, melted and cooled
1 large egg, lightly beaten

Filling:
6 tablespoons unsalted butter, softened
⅓ cup firmly packed light brown sugar
1½ tablespoons ground cinnamon
¼ teaspoon ground nutmeg

Glaze:
½ (8-ounce) package cream cheese, softened
2½ cups confectioners' sugar, sifted
2 tablespoons heavy whipping cream
½ teaspoon vanilla extract

1. Spray a 5- to 6-quart slow cooker with cooking spray. Line slow cooker with parchment paper, trimming edges of paper just below rim. Spray parchment with cooking spray.

2. For dough: In the bowl of a stand mixer fitted with the whisk attachment, place warm milk and honey. Gently stir in yeast, and let stand for 5 minutes.

3. In a medium bowl, whisk together flour, sugar, and salt. With mixer on low speed, gradually add flour mixture to milk mixture, beating just until combined. Add melted butter and egg; beat just until a dough forms. Switch to the dough hook attachment; beat at medium speed until dough is smooth and elastic, 5 to 7 minutes.

4. For filling: On a lightly floured surface, roll dough into a 15x9-inch rectangle. Spread butter onto dough. In a small bowl, stir together brown sugar, cinnamon, and nutmeg. Sprinkle sugar mixture over butter. Starting with one long side, roll dough into a log; pinch seam to seal. Slice into 12 rolls. Place rolls in slow cooker.

5. Cover and cook on high for 2 hours. Using the parchment as handles, carefully lift cinnamon rolls from slow cooker insert.

6. For glaze: In a large bowl, beat cream cheese with a mixer at medium-high speed until creamy. Gradually add confectioners' sugar, beating until smooth. Add cream and vanilla, beating just until combined. Drizzle glaze over rolls.

Pineapple-Strawberry Upside-Down Cake

Strawberries add a punch of color and bright flavor to this classic cake.

MAKES 8 TO 10 SERVINGS

1 cup firmly packed light brown sugar

¼ cup unsalted butter, melted

1 (20-ounce) can sliced pineapple, juice reserved

1 (16-ounce) container frozen strawberries in syrup, thawed

1 (15.25-ounce) box yellow cake mix*

4 large eggs

⅓ cup vegetable oil

1. Spray a 5- to 6-quart slow cooker with cooking spray.

2. In a small bowl, stir together brown sugar and melted butter; spread in bottom of slow cooker.

3. Cut each pineapple ring into 4 pieces. Place pieces in a single layer over brown sugar mixture. Spoon strawberries and syrup over pineapple.

4. In a large bowl, beat cake mix, eggs, oil, and reserved pineapple juice with a mixer at medium speed until combined, about 2 minutes. Pour into slow cooker.

5. Cover and cook on high until a wooden pick inserted in center comes out clean, about 2 hours. Remove slow cooker insert, and let cool on a wire rack for 1 hour. Place a serving plate over insert, and carefully invert cake onto plate.

We used Duncan Hines.

Sundries

THESE EASY RECIPES FOR DIPS, SNACKS,
AND CONDIMENTS SHOW HOW VERSATILE
YOUR SLOW COOKER CAN BE

Balsamic Ketchup

This homemade ketchup beats store-bought versions any day.

MAKES ABOUT 5½ CUPS

1   **tablespoon canola oil**

1   **cup finely chopped red onion**

2   **(28-ounce) cans tomato purée**

1   **(28-ounce) can plum tomatoes, drained and chopped**

¾   **cup firmly packed light brown sugar**

¾   **cup balsamic vinegar**

1   **tablespoon minced fresh rosemary**

2   **teaspoons minced fresh garlic**

¼   **teaspoon kosher salt**

1. In a small skillet, heat oil over medium-high heat. Add onion; cook until lightly browned, about 3 minutes. Transfer to a 5-quart slow cooker. Add tomato purée and remaining ingredients.

2. Cover and cook on low until thickened and bubbly, about 11 hours, or on high for 5 hours. Spoon into a bowl, and let cool completely. Cover and refrigerate up to 2 weeks.

Slow Cooker Snack Mix

Don't skip the liquid smoke in this snack mix—it adds a hint of smoky flavor.

MAKES 12 SERVINGS

2   cups toasted corn cereal
2   cups toasted rice cereal
2   cups toasted wheat cereal
2   cups toasted whole grain oat cereal
2   cups pretzels
1   cup dry roasted peanuts
1   cup roasted almonds
½   cup unsalted butter, melted
¼   cup firmly packed light brown sugar
1   tablespoon kosher salt
1   teaspoon garlic powder
1   teaspoon smoked paprika
¼   teaspoon ground red pepper
⅓   cup chopped fresh rosemary
¼   cup Worcestershire sauce
1   teaspoon liquid smoke

1. Spray the insert of a 6-quart slow cooker with cooking spray; add cereals, pretzels, peanuts, and almonds.
2. In a medium bowl, whisk together melted butter, sugar, salt, garlic powder, paprika, and red pepper; stir until sugar dissolves. Add rosemary, Worcestershire, and liquid smoke. Pour butter mixture over cereal mixture; stir to combine.
3. Cover and cook on low for 3 hours, stirring every 45 minutes. Line rimmed baking sheets with parchment paper. Spread snack mix in an even layer on prepared pans. Let stand at room temperature until dry, about 30 minutes. Store in an airtight container for up to 3 weeks.

Spiced Pear Butter

Spooned over biscuits or drizzled on ice cream, this pear butter adds rich fall flavor.

MAKES ABOUT 4 CUPS

12   Bartlett pears, peeled and chopped (about 2½ pounds)
½   cup apple cider vinegar
½   cup cane syrup
2   tablespoons fresh lemon juice
1   tablespoon vanilla extract
2   cups firmly packed light brown sugar
2   tablespoons ground cinnamon
1   tablespoon ground cardamom
2   teaspoons ground allspice
1   teaspoon kosher salt
½   teaspoon ground cloves
¼   teaspoon ground nutmeg

1. In a 5-quart slow cooker, stir together pears and remaining ingredients.
2. Cover and cook on high for 6 to 8 hours, stirring every hour. Using a potato masher, finely mash pears.
3. Cover and cook on low for 6 hours.
4. In the container of a blender, purée pear mixture until smooth. Transfer to airtight containers. Refrigerate for up to 2 weeks.

Corn-Jalapeño Queso Dip

This spicy dip is the perfect game-day appetizer.

MAKES 8 TO 10 SERVINGS

6   cups yellow corn kernels
1   red bell pepper, diced
2   fresh jalapeño peppers, seeded
     and diced
2   tablespoons minced
     fresh chives
2   tablespoons minced
     fresh cilantro
1   teaspoon minced garlic
1   (8-ounce) package white
     Cheddar cheese, shredded
1   (8-ounce) package cream
     cheese, cubed
1   cup shredded Monterey Jack
     cheese with peppers
½   cup sour cream
1½   teaspoons kosher salt
1   teaspoon ground black pepper
⅓   cup cooked crumbled bacon
Tortilla chips, to serve
Garnish: chopped green onion

1. In a 4-quart slow cooker, stir together corn, bell pepper, jalapeño, chives, cilantro, and garlic. Stir in Cheddar, cream cheese, Monterey Jack, and sour cream.
2. Cover and cook on high for 2 hours, stirring every 45 minutes. Season with salt and pepper. Stir in bacon. Serve with chips. Garnish with green onion, if desired.

Pimiento Cheese Dip

The South's favorite spread gets a makeover with this slow cooker recipe.

MAKES ABOUT 10 SERVINGS

1   pound cubed processed cheese*
3   (4-ounce) jars diced
     pimientos, undrained
1   (8-ounce) package finely
     shredded sharp Cheddar cheese
2   tablespoons mayonnaise
2   tablespoons whole milk
2   teaspoons smoked
     paprika, divided
1½ teaspoons hot sauce
½   teaspoon garlic powder
Saltine crackers, celery sticks,
     bell pepper strips, to serve

1. In a 2-quart slow cooker, combine processed cheese and pimientos.
2. Cover and cook on low for 40 minutes or until melted, stirring occasionally. Whisk in Cheddar, mayonnaise, milk, 1½ teaspoons paprika, hot sauce, and garlic powder.
3. Cook until heated through, about 15 minutes. Sprinkle with remaining ½ teaspoon paprika. Serve with crackers, celery, and bell pepper.

We used Velveeta.

Slow Cooker Chai Lattes

With cardamom, cinnamon, and ginger, this cozy tea will be your new winter warm-up.

MAKES ABOUT 8 SERVINGS

3 quarts simmering water
12 regular black tea bags
4 star anise
3 tablespoons black peppercorns
3 tablespoons cardamom pods
4 cinnamon sticks, halved
4 slices fresh ginger
2 (3-inch) strips orange zest
1 (14-ounce) can sweetened condensed milk
2 tablespoons sugar
Garnish: orange zest strips, ground cinnamon

1. In a 5-quart slow cooker, combine 3 quarts simmering water and tea bags. Cover and let stand for 8 minutes. Discard tea bags.

2. In a heavy-duty resealable bag, combine star anise, peppercorns, and cardamom pods. Seal bag; pound with a rolling pin until coarsely crushed.

3. Place peppercorn mixture, cinnamon sticks, ginger, and zest on a 6-inch-square piece of cheesecloth. Bring edges of cheesecloth together to completely enclose spices; tie with kitchen twine. Add cheesecloth bundle to slow cooker.

4. Cover and cook on low for 2 hours. Discard cheesecloth bundle. Stir in sweetened condensed milk and sugar. Garnish servings with zest strips and cinnamon, if desired.

Chili Cheese Dip

Bring this dip to your next gathering—your friends and family will love you for it.

MAKES 2½ QUARTS

1   **pound lean ground beef**
½   **cup diced yellow onion**
1   **poblano pepper, seeded and diced (about ½ cup)**
1   **tablespoon minced garlic**
1   **(1.25-ounce) package chili seasoning mix**
1   **(15-ounce) can black beans, drained and rinsed**
1   **(10-ounce) can diced tomatoes with green chiles**
1½   **pounds yellow American cheese, cut into ½-inch pieces**
2   **cups half-and-half, divided**
Garnish: diced poblano pepper
Corn chips, to serve

1. Spray a 3- to 4-quart slow cooker with cooking spray.

2. In a large nonstick skillet, cook beef, onion, poblano, and garlic over medium-high heat, stirring frequently, until meat is browned and onions are tender; drain. Stir in chili seasoning mix. Transfer mixture to slow cooker. Stir in beans, tomatoes with green chiles, cheese, and 1½ cups half-and-half.

3. Cover and cook on low, stirring occasionally, until melted and smooth, 3 to 4 hours. Stir in remaining ½ cup half-and-half to thin, if desired. Garnish with poblano, if desired. Serve with corn chips.

Chicken and Spinach Artichoke Dip

Appetizers don't get much easier than this set-it-and-forget-it dip.

MAKES ABOUT 10 SERVINGS

3 (8-ounce) packages cream cheese, softened

2 cooked boneless skinless chicken breasts, shredded

1 (14-ounce) can quartered artichoke hearts, drained and chopped

1 (10-ounce) package frozen chopped spinach, thawed and squeezed dry

1½ cups whole milk, divided

1 cup shredded mozzarella cheese

1 tablespoon minced fresh garlic

1 teaspoon Italian seasoning

¼ teaspoon crushed red pepper

Crostini, to serve

1. Spray a 3- to 4-quart slow cooker with cooking spray.

2. Add cream cheese, chicken, artichoke hearts, spinach, 1 cup milk, mozzarella, garlic, Italian seasoning, and red pepper to slow cooker. Stir to combine.

3. Cover and cook on high until cheese is melted, 1 to 2 hours, stirring every 30 minutes. Stir in remaining ½ cup milk to thin, if desired. Serve hot with crostini.

TO MAKE CROSTINI: Preheat oven to 350°. Place baguette slices on a large rimmed baking sheet. Brush both sides with oil; sprinkle with salt and pepper. Bake until slightly crispy, 6 to 10 minutes.

recipe index